ADHD Managem
Older Women

Uncovering The Hidden Secrets, Symptoms, Diagnosis, And Treatment Of Attention Deficit Hyperactivity Disorder In Women

Written by:

Jennifer Sorensen

Copyright © 2022 – By Jennifer Sorensen

Disclaimer Notice:

We put forth a lot of effort to ensure that the information we provide to you is reliable, based on the opinion of experts, and as current as possible. This book is solely intended to serve as a source of general information. It is not intended to replace independent, professional medical or health advice that has been adapted to your unique circumstances and should not be considered such. If you are having issues of a psychological kind, we strongly advise you to go for assistance from a qualified source as soon as possible.

TABLE OF CONTENT

Overview and Facts

What Is ADHD?

Attention Deficit Hyperactivity Disorder is a neurodevelopmental disorder defined by the American Psychiatric Association (APA). ADHD is diagnosed in children and adults based on symptoms of inattention and hyperactivity-impulsivity. While it's true that everyone experiences ADHD symptoms from time to time, they vary in severity and not everyone has ADHD.

People with ADHD often have difficulty performing daily tasks and are at greater risk for negative life outcomes such as divorce, job loss, accidents, and substance abuse. At the same time, many people with ADHD thrive on the unique functioning of their brains. ADHD can also be a lack of creativity, curiosity, the ability to take risks, and the ability to think outside the box.

ADHD And Women

- 50-75% of women and girls with ADHD do not know they have ADHD and are consistently unrecognized and underdiagnosed.
- Symptoms of inattention are more common than symptoms of hyperactivity and impulsivity in girls and women with ADHD.
- Women with ADHD are more likely to have low self-esteem and more anxiety and depression than men with ADHD and women without ADHD.
- Anxiety and mood disorders often coexist with ADHD in women, who are more likely to have phobias and generalized anxiety disorder than in men with ADHD.
- Men are three times more likely to have ADHD than women, and because women and non-binary ADHD

sufferers are often overlooked or misdiagnosed, it is common for them to be diagnosed later in life when life spirals out of control.

Why ADHD Is Underdiagnosed In Girls, Women, And Nonbinary People

Girls have ADHD just as much as boys, but boys are diagnosed much more often than girls. This is usually due to the way their ADHD manifests and gender bias in the diagnosis of ADHD. Boys are more likely than girls to have behavioral problems, while girls are more likely to be apathetic or have a co-occurring mood disorder.

Why do girls have such different symptoms? Experts like Dr. Kathleen Nadeau, director of the Chesapeake ADHD Center, suggest this is partly due to differences in socialization. Symptoms in girls are often due to gender stereotypes and can be overlooked.

Our culture encourages girls to be more socially conscious, and they are expected to perform and behave well. This may explain why even if a girl has undiagnosed ADHD symptoms, such as disorganization, distraction, and forgetfulness, her symptoms may go unnoticed due to her social and cultural awareness.

An example of this is a girl with undiagnosed ADHD who procrastinates while writing an article. She would probably finish it at the last minute and turn it in. This is compared to a boy with undiagnosed ADHD who also procrastinated to write the same article but didn't feel the added social and cultural pressure to complete and submit the article on time.

In this situation, the boy's hyperactive-impulsive ADHD presentation would be more likely to be affected and therefore detectable compared to the girl's attentive ADHD presentation. This is an example of how girls can slip through the cracks.

Girls with ADHD are at greater risk than boys, and the condition can affect girls' emotional health, self-esteem, and general well-being. The girl in the example above may get a good grade on the paper, but because she had to work three times as hard to get it, she still sees herself as worthless, incompetent, and not as smart as she should be.

"It is common for women whose ADHD was overlooked when they were young to be given an anxiety or depressive disorder diagnosis later in life. It is typical for an individual to receive an ADHD diagnosis only after undergoing therapy for anxiety and depression".

Society has certain expectations that we place on women, and ADHD often makes it difficult to meet those expectations. They need to be the organizer, planner, and primary parent in the home. Women are expected to remember birthdays and anniversaries, do laundry and keep track of events. It's hard for someone with ADHD.

Symptoms

ADHD diagnoses are divided into three presentations: *primary attention deficit, primary hyperactive-impulsive, and combined.* It is important to note that there are different levels of difficulty.

Attention Deficit Presentation

- Cannot pay attention to detail or make careless mistakes

- Difficult to maintain attention
- Doesn't seem to be listening
- Difficulty following instructions
- Difficult to organize
- Steer clear of or detest things that need constant mental effort
- Loses things
- Easily distracted
- Is forgetful in daily activities

Hyperactive-Impulsive Presentation

- Wriggles with arms or legs or squirms in a chair
- Difficulty sitting
- runs or climbs too much with children; extreme restlessness in adults
- Difficulty in play activities
- Works as if driven by a motor; Adults often feel driven by a motor inside
- Talk too much
- Hides answers before questions are ready
- Difficulty waiting or taking turns

- Interrupts or disturbs others

ADHD Combined Presentation

The person meets the criteria for both attentive and hyperactive-impulsive ADHD presentations.

Other ADHD Symptoms In Women

- Overcommitting, overworking, overthinking, over-planning and over-performing
- Consistent comparison
- Take care of others without taking time for yourself
- Constant feeling of overload and exhaustion
- Low self-esteem
- Depression and anxiety
- Time management issues - how much time has passed or how much time is needed
- Sleep disturbances and constant fatigue
- Being Withdrawn
- inattention or tendency to "daydream"
- feeling of inadequacy

- Higher risk of suicidal thoughts
- Hyperfocus
- Perfectionism
- Procrastination

How To Know If You Need To Be Tested

Most people who seek an ADHD evaluation have significant problems in many areas of their lives, including home, school, and work. If you're having trouble getting through your day, it might be time to test yourself. Take time to learn about the signs and symptoms, think back to your formative years, and talk to a trusted friend or mental health professional.

Diagnosis

I do not group or categorize people, and I recognize the additional pain that misdiagnosis can cause, especially for older women, non-binary people, and BIPOC communities. I also know that receiving a diagnosis can be a great asset and inform the treatment plan.

Getting a professional diagnosis is a privilege. Women and non-binary people are affected by ADHD in ways that men (especially white men) are not. Black and POC women and children are also at a much higher risk of not being diagnosed and as a result, there are now overwhelming numbers of women and non-binary people who are only now finding out that they may have ADHD.

Getting tested and diagnosed can be overwhelming and mentally draining, and I recognize that not everyone is privileged to receive the support they deserve.

A diagnosis requires at least six symptoms that cross age. Symptoms must persist for more than six months and must be present before age 40 and not be better accounted for by another medical condition.

Why You Should Get Diagnosis And Treatment And How Will This Affect You?

The goal of diagnosis and treatment is to help people become more efficient in their daily lives and to reduce the extent to which their untreated ADHD affects functioning and general well-being.

Proper diagnosis and treatment can help get to the root of the problem, especially if you have been misdiagnosed. It can also help you defend yourself and your needs, e.g., when finding the right accommodation for work and school.

What To Expect If ADHD Is Untreated

Untreated ADHD is associated with many problems, including substance abuse, higher divorce rates, higher unemployment risks, problems at work and school, etc. Untreated women are more likely to suffer from depression, anxiety, low self-esteem, and greater suicidal thoughts.

People who are undiagnosed often feel restless, frustrated, and unable to understand what is happening to them. Undiagnosed women are sometimes constantly compared to other women due to social and cultural pressures on women and women seem controlled, organized, focused, and alert.

While getting a diagnosis is one way to access all treatment options, more often than not it helps people understand, accept, and even appreciate their unique brain functioning.

Chapter 1.

Understanding The ADHD Brain

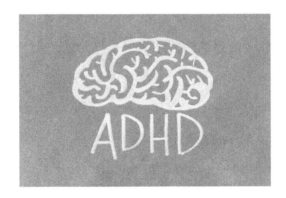

M ost people are neurologically wired to figure out what's important and are motivated to do it, even if they don't care. Then the rest of us with attention deficit disorder – ADHD or ADD – and the brains that come with it.

Attention Deficit Hyperactivity Disorder is a confusing, contradictory, conflicted, and frustrating condition. It's overwhelming for people who live with it every day. The diagnostic criteria used over the past 40 years have caused many people to wonder whether or not they have the disease. Diagnosing physicians have a long list of symptoms to study and monitor. The Diagnostic and Statistical Manual of Mental Disorders has 18 criteria and other symptom lists have up to 100 characteristics.

Practitioners, myself included, have tried to find an easier and clearer way to understand the limitations of ADHD. We are looking for a "clear and bright line" that defines the condition, explains the cause of the disturbances, and advises what to do about it.

My work over the past decade suggests that we are missing something important about the fundamental nature of the ADHD brain. I went back to experts 0n the condition, the hundreds of people I had worked with who had been diagnosed, and their families to confirm my hypothesis. My intention was to look for a trait that all individuals with ADHD have but that neurotypical individuals do not.

I found it. This is the ADHD nervous system, a unique and special creation that regulates attention and emotions differently from the nervous system of people without the disorder.

The ADHD Zone

Almost all of my patients and their families want to get rid of the term ADHD because it describes the opposite of what they are going through every moment of their lives. It's hard to call something a disorder when it has so many positive aspects. ADHD is not a damaged or defective nervous system. It is a nervous system that functions well according to its own rules.

Despite ADHD's association with learning disabilities, most people with ADHD have significantly higher-than-average IQs. They also use higher IQs differently from neurotypical people. By the time most people with this condition get to high school, they are able to face the problems everyone else is facing and leap to solutions no one else has seen.

Most adults with an ADHD neurological system do not exhibit overt hyperactivity. They have internal hyperactivity. There is no lack of attention for those with the disorder. Most people with non-drug ADHD have four or five things on their minds at once. The hallmark of the attention deficit hyperactivity disorder system is not attention, but inconsistent attention.

Anyone with ADHD knows they can "find themselves in the zone" at least four or five times a day. Once in the zone, they no longer have limits, and all the executive function deficits they had before entering the zone disappear.

People with ADHD know they are smart and smart, but they never know if their skills will show up when they need them. The distinguishing feature of ADHD is that symptoms and deficits change throughout the course of the day. It obscures and frustrates the condition.

People with ADHD usually enter the zone being interested or fascinated by what they are doing. I call it the **interest-based nervous system.** Judged friends and family members see this as untrustworthy or selfish. When friends say, "You can do whatever you want," they're describing the essence of the ADHD nervous system.

ADHD individuals also fail when challenged or thrown into a competitive environment. Sometimes a new or novel task catches their attention. However, the messages are short and everything times out after a while.

Most people with ADHD can complete tasks and use their skills when the task is urgent, such as a deadline. This is why procrastination is almost a common disorder among ADHD patients. They want the job done, but can't get started until the task becomes interesting, difficult, or urgent.

How The Rest Of The World Works

90% of people in the world without ADHD are considered "neurotypical". It's not like they're "normal" or better. Their neurology is accepted and recognized by the world. For people with a neurotypical nervous system, being interested in the task or being challenged, or finding a new or urgent task helps, but it doesn't have to be.

Neurotypical people use three different factors to decide what to do, how to do it, and stick with it until it's done:

1. the concept of importance (they think they should get it done).
2. The concept of secondary importance, they are motivated by the fact that their parents, teachers, principals or

someone they respect thinks it is important to take on and complete the task.

3. The concept of reward for completing a task and consequences/punishments for failure.

A person with ADHD nervous system has never been able to use the idea of meaning or rewards to initiate and accomplish a task. They know what's important, they like rewards, and they don't like punishments. But to them, the things that motivate the rest of the world are just bullshit.

The inability to motivate oneself with meaning and rewards has a lifelong impact on the lives of people with ADHD:

- How can people diagnosed with ADHD choose between options when they cannot use the concepts of importance and financial reward to motivate them?
- How can they make good decisions if the concepts of importance and reward don't help them make a decision or motivate them to do what they choose?

This finding explains why none of the cognitive behavioral therapies used to treat ADHD symptoms have any lasting benefit.

Researchers see ADHD as the result of a faulty or impaired nervous system. I see ADHD as the result of a perfectly functioning nervous system on its own terms. Unfortunately, it doesn't work according to the rules or techniques taught and encouraged in a neurotypical world. For this reason:

- People with ADHD don't fit into the traditional school system of repeating what others find important and relevant.
- People with ADHD don't thrive in a standard job that pays people to work on something important for someone else (namely, the boss).
- People with ADHD are disorganized because almost all organizational systems are based on two things – prioritization and time management – that people with ADHD are not good at.
- People with ADHD struggle to make decisions due to a similar lack of value in all options, they see no difference between the options.
- People with ADHD nervous system know that if they focus on a task, they can do it. Far from being damaged goods, people with ADHD nervous system are smart and

intelligent. The main problem is that they were given a neurotypical manual at birth. It works for everyone, not for her.

People With ADHD Are Not Neurotypical People

The implications of this new understanding are enormous. The first is to get coaches, doctors, and professionals to stop turning people with ADHD into neurotypical people. The goal should be to intervene as soon as possible before the individual becomes frustrated and demoralized by struggling in a neurotypical world where the game is against them. A therapeutic approach that has a chance of success like no other must consist of two parts:

Leveling the neurological playing field with medication so that the person with ADHD has focus, impulse control, and the ability to stay calm on the inside. For most people, this requires two different medications.

Stimulants improve the day-to-day performance of people with ADHD and help them get things done. They are not effective in calming the internal over-excitement that many people with ADHD experience. For these symptoms, the majority of people benefit from adding one of the alpha agonists (guanfacine/Intuniv or clonidine/Kapvay) to the stimulant.

However, ADHD medications are not enough. A person can take the right drug at the right dose, but nothing changes if he pursues his tasks with neurotypical strategies.

The second part of ADHD symptom management is to have a person create their own ADHD user guide. The generic user manuals that have been written are disappointing for people with this condition. Like everyone else, people with ADHD grow and mature over time. What interests and challenges a child of seven will no longer interest and challenge him at 27.

Make Your Own Rules

The ADHD user manual should be based on current successes. How do you enter the zone now? Under what circumstances are you successful and happy in your current life? Instead of focusing on the weak points, figure out how to get into the zone and perform at an outstanding level.

I usually suggest that my patients take a notepad or tape recorder with them for a month to write down or explain how they get into the zone.

Because they are interested? If so, what fascinates you most about the task or situation?

Is it because they feel competitive? If so, what about the "adversary" or the situation brings out the competing forces?

By the end of the month, most people will have collected 50 or 60 different techniques that they know work for them. When asked to watch and participate, they now understand how their nervous system works and what techniques help them.

I've seen these strategies work for many people with ADHD because they took a step back and discovered the triggers, they needed to overcome them. This approach does not try to make people with ADHD neurotypical (as if that were possible) but offers lifelong help because it builds on their strengths.

Chapter 2.

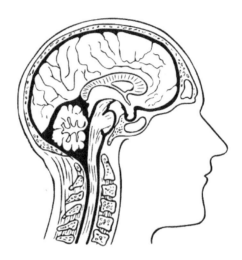

How Older Adults With ADHD Think: Unfair Truths About The ADHD Nervous System

E asily bored, prone to distraction, creative, and intense. If you grew up with ADHD symptoms, chances are you've always felt "different." Here is a scientific explanation of the neurological basis of behavior and emotions associated with Attention Deficit Hyperactivity Disorder.

Here's a truth people with Attention Deficit Hyperactivity Disorder (ADHD or ADD) have known since childhood: If you have ADHD nervous system, you might as well have been born on another planet.

Most individuals with ADHD have always been aware of their unique style of thinking. They were told by their parents, teachers, employers, spouses, and friends that they didn't fit the mold and that if they wanted to do something on their own, it was best to get in shape fast.

As if they were immigrants, they were told to adapt to the dominant culture and become like everyone else. Unfortunately, no one told them how to do it. Nobody revealed the biggest secret: it was not possible, no matter how hard they tried. The only outcome would be a failure, with the accusation that they will never succeed because adult ADHD means they haven't tried hard enough or long enough.

It seems strange to call a condition when the condition has so many positive characteristics. People with an ADHD-type nervous system are generally good problem solvers. They delve into problems that everyone is worried about and find the answer.

They are friendly, sympathetic people with a sense of humor. They have what *Paul Wender* called "ruthless determination". When faced with a challenge, they take on one approach at a time until they have mastered the situation and they can lose interest completely when it is no longer a challenge.

If I could name the qualities that guarantee success in life, I would say being intelligent, being creative with that intelligence, and being loving. I would choose diligent and hardworking. I wish I had many of the qualities that people with ADHD have.

The main obstacle to understanding and treating ADHD is the tacit and incorrect assumption that people with ADHD can and should be like all of us. For neurotypical people and adults with ADHD, here's a detailed look at why people with ADHD do what they do.

Why people with ADHD don't function well in a linear world

The world of ADHD is curvilinear. Past, present, and future are never separate and different. it's all now People with ADHD live in a constant presence and find it difficult to learn from the past or look to the future to see the inevitable consequences of their actions. "Acting without thinking" is the definition of impulsivity and one of the reasons people with ADHD have trouble learning from experience.

It also means that people with ADHD are not good at ordering – planning and doing parts of a task in the correct order. In the neurotypical world, tasks have a start, middle, and finish. People with ADHD don't know where and how to start because they can't find the beginning. You jump in the middle of a task and work in all directions at the same time. Organizing becomes an unsustainable task because organizational systems operate with linearity, meaning, and time.

Why People With ADHD Are Overwhelmed

People in the ADHD world live life more intensely, more passionately than neurotypical people. They have a low threshold for external sensory experiences because the daily experience of their five senses and thoughts is always at high volume. The ADHD nervous system is overwhelmed with life experiences because the intensity is so high.

The ADHD nervous system is rarely at rest. It wants to do something interesting and challenging. Attention is never "deficit". it is always excessive, constantly occupied with inner dreams and obligations. When people with ADHD are out of the zone, in hyperfocus, they have four or five things on their minds at once for no apparent reason, like five people talking to you at once. Nothing gets sustained undivided attention. Nothing is done well.

Many people with ADHD are unable to filter sensory input. Sometimes it refers to a single sensory world, such as hearing. In fact, the phenomenon is called hyperacusis (amplified hearing), even if the limitation comes from another of the five senses. Here are some examples:

- The slightest noise in the house keeps you from falling asleep and overwhelms the ability to ignore it.
- Any movement, no matter how small, is a distraction.
- Certain smells that others barely notice cause people with ADHD to leave the room.

In people with ADHD, their world is constantly disrupted by experiences of which the neurotypical person is unaware. This condition forces the perception of the ADHD person as strange, thorny, demanding, and demanding. But that's all-ADHD sufferers have ever experienced. It is his normality. The idea of being different, and that the difference is perceived as unacceptable by others, becomes part of how they are perceived. It is part of their identity.

Sometimes someone with ADHD can meet deadlines and produce a lot of high-quality work in a short time. An entire semester of study is wrapped up in a night of hyper-focused perfection. Some people with ADHD create seizures to generate the adrenaline needed to make them function. The 'masters of disasters' handle high-intensity crises with ease, only to crumble when things get back to routine.

However, moving from crisis to crisis is a difficult way of life. Sometimes I meet people who use anger to get the adrenaline rush they need to be engaged and productive. They invoke resentment or contempt from years ago to motivate themselves. The price they pay for their productivity is so high that they can be considered to have personality disorders.

Why People With ADHD Can't Always Get Things Done

People with ADHD are both baffled and frustrated by the secrets of the ADHD brain, which is its intermittent ability to be super focused when interested, and challenged and unable to initiate and sustain personally boring projects.

It's not that they don't want to get things done or that they can't do the job. They know they are capable and capable because they have proven it over and over.

The lifelong frustration is never being sure that they will be able to participate when needed when others depend on them. When people with ADHD view themselves as unreliable, they begin to doubt their talents and become ashamed of being unreliable.

Mood and energy levels also vary with interest and challenge. When the person with ADHD is bored, inattentive, or stuck on a task, they are lethargic, argumentative, and full of discontent.

Why Our ADHD Motors Always Run

By the time most people with ADHD are teenagers, their physical hyperactivity is suppressed and hidden. But it is there and it still hinders the ability to live in the present, to listen to others, to relax enough to fall asleep at night and have periods of rest.

So when distraction and impulsivity are brought back to normal levels by stimulant medication, a person with ADHD may not be able to use their calm state. It is always fed as if by an engine from within, hidden from the rest of the world. By adolescence, most people with ADHD-like nervous systems have learned the social skills needed to hide their absence.

But they rarely come out completely. While they tune in to what's going on, while they're lost in thought, the world has gone on without them. Oops. They are lost and don't know what is happening, what they missed, and what is expected of them now.

Their return to the neurotypical world is unpleasant and disorienting. For people with ADHD, the outside world isn't as bright as the fantastic ideas they had when they were lost in their own thoughts.

Why the organization shuns people with ADHD

The ADHD mind is a vast, disorganized library. It contains a lot of information in fragments, but not whole books. Information comes in many forms - such as articles, videos, audio clips, and web pages- as well as forms and thoughts that no one had before. But there is no card catalog and the "books" are not organized by subject or even alphabetically.

Each person with ADHD has their own brain library and their own way of storing the vast amount of material. No wonder the average person with ADHD can't access the right information when they need it - there's no reliable mechanism to locate it.

Important objects (God help us, important to someone else) have no fixed location and can be invisible or completely absent. For instance: A kid with ADHD comes home and tells their mom there's no homework. He watches television or plays video games until he goes to bed.

Then he thinks he has a bigger report in the morning. Is the child deliberately lying to the parents or was he really unaware of the importance of the task? For someone with ADHD, there is a lack of information and memories that are not visible. Your mind is a computer in RAM, with no reliable access to information on the disk.

Working memory is the ability to hold data in your head and manipulate it to arrive at an answer or plan of action. The mind of someone with ADHD is full of the details of life ("Where are my keys?", "Where did I park the car?"), limiting the space for fresh ideas and recollections. To create a way for new knowledge, something must be eliminated or forgotten. People with ADHD often have the knowledge they need someplace in their memory. Simply said, it is not in demand.

Why We Don't See Ourselves Clearly

People in the ADHD world have low self-esteem. Although they are often good at reading others, it is difficult for the average person with ADHD to know at all times how they are feeling, the effect they are having on others, and what they are feeling. Neurotypical people misinterpret it as emotional, narcissistic, indifferent, or socially inadequate. In general, a person with ADHD's sensitivity to negative feedback from others and an inability to observe themselves at the moment creates a witch bridge.

If a person cannot see what is happening, the feedback loop through which they learn is broken. If a person doesn't know what's wrong or in what specific way it's wrong, then they don't know how to fix it. If people with ADHD don't know what they're doing, they don't do it anymore.

The ADHD mind's inability to recognize what is going on has many consequences:

Many people with ADHD find that the feedback they receive from others is different from what they see. They often discover (and often too late) that others were always right. Only when something is wrong can they see and understand what was obvious to everyone else. Then they believe they can't trust their own perception of what's going on. They lose confidence. Despite their commitment, many people with ADHD never know if they are doing something right.

ADHD patients may not understand the benefits of medications, even if they are obvious. If the patient does not see the problems of ADHD or the benefits of treatment, they will not find a reason to continue treatment. People who have ADHD may feel unjustly accused, worthless, and misunderstood. One recurring topic is alienation. Most people believe that only another person with ADHD "gets" them.

Why do people with ADHD have little time

Because ADHD patients don't have a reliable sense of time, it's all happening now or not at all. Along with the concept of sanctification (what to do first, what to do next), there is also the concept of time. The things at the top of the list should be done first, and time should be allowed to complete the whole task.

I found that 85% of my ADHD patients don't wear or own a watch. More than half of those who wore a watch did not wear it, but wore it as jewelry or to avoid hurting the person who gave it to them. Time is a meaningless notion to those with ADHD. Even though it could be significant to others, persons with ADHD seldom understand it.

Chapter 3.

Why ADHD In Women Is Routinely Dismissed, Misdiagnosed, And Treated Inadequately

Attention Deficit Hyperactivity Disorder is not a male disease, but men and boys are diagnosed much more often than women and girls. Why? Persistent stereotypes, referral biases, internalized symptoms, gender role expectations, comorbidities, and hormonal fluctuations complicate the presentation of ADHD in women.

ADHD is a neurological condition marked by a recurring pattern of inattention that interferes with everyday functioning, whether or not it is accompanied by hyperactivity and impulsivity. Although the prevalence is more proportional by gender, the rate of diagnosis among American men is almost 69% higher than among American women (5.4% of American men are diagnosed with ADHD compared to only 3.2% of American women).

Why? ADHD in women does not fit the stereotypes. The apparent presentation of symptoms is skewed toward inattention, a feature that partly explains why ADHD in women is widely misunderstood, overlooked, and understudied.

Despite increased awareness of ADHD in general, science still has much to learn and discover about ADHD in women, especially the impact of biology, neurology, and gender concepts on the condition's appearance, and the course of treatment.

ADHD in women: historical perspectives

Our understanding of ADHD has evolved considerably. Once considered a condition defined by measures of hyperactivity in children, ADHD is now considered inattentive and can last a lifetime. However, many outdated stereotypes about ADHD exist inside and outside of the medical community, which hampers the research, detection, and treatment of ADHD in women today. New research predicts serious mental and physical health consequences for women who are underestimated and undertreated due to harmful ADHD myths such as:

- ADHD is a male disorder. Hyperactive boys, considered disruptive and out of control, were referred to clinics. Early studies were based on the behavior of these hyperactive white boys; These findings helped form the diagnostic criteria and rating scales that are still used today.

- ADHD is a childhood disease. ADHD has long been classified as a disruptive behavior disorder in children based on the characteristic of hyperactivity. Over time, it has become apparent that ADHD does not progress until adolescence and that undetected symptom last longer than hyperactivity symptoms.

Signs And Symptoms

ADHD in women primarily means a higher chance of the following:

- inattentive symptom presentation, including, per the DSM-5
- not paying attention to details or making careless mistakes in business
- Difficulty paying attention to tasks
- not following instructions and not completing tasks (e.g., losing concentration, stopping)
- Difficulty organizing tasks and activities
- easily disturbed
- forgetfulness in daily activities
- Internalizing symptoms, including moodiness and anxiety.

Gender Role Expectations

Gender role expectations complicate ADHD in women. The long list of expectations that society places on women - the care of themselves, the family, and the household necessitates a coherent coordination of executive functions.

ADHD women are ill-equipped to meet these demands. However, in their quest for social acceptance, they often choose to hide it, usually by masking symptoms and problems. Shame and self-blame fuel the dynamic interplay between societal expectations and ADHD dysfunction. To understand women with ADHD, clinicians should not underestimate the extent to which women measure their self-worth and self-worth by their ability to meet gender expectations.

Social Deficits

Compared to men with ADHD, women with ADHD have more difficulty socializing.

- Women are often caught up in the demands of relationships and as a result, have less meaningful relationships. They rarely start friendships and find it difficult to maintain them. Isolation protects against discomfort and confusion.
- They often struggle with rejection sensitivity, a strong emotional response to real or perceived rejection, which can make social interaction a potential source of pain.

- They are more likely to engage in risky sexual behaviors than women without ADHD. One theory on this is the early recognition of sexuality as a shortcut to social acceptance. Women with ADHD often had earlier sexual activity, earlier sex, more sexual partners, more casual sex, less safe sex, more sexually transmitted diseases, and more unplanned pregnancies. Although these experiences are common, some aspects of ADHD evoke shame.

Hypersensitivity

Women with ADHD tend to experience more central nervous system hypersensitivity than men with ADHD. They often yield more of the following:

- tactile defense and sensory overload (touch and common objects such as clothing, stickers, loud music, lights, smells, etc.)
- physical complaints, including headaches, migraine, abdominal pain, and nausea
- sleep problems

Comorbidities

By adulthood, most women with ADHD have at least one comorbid condition that can complicate the picture of ADHD symptoms, including:

- Anxiety (25-40% of people with ADHD have an anxiety disorder)
- mood disorders
- eating disorder (bulimia is the most common)
- externalizing disorders such as oppositional defiant disorder (ODD) or conduct disorder (usually in women with impulsive ADHD)
- personality disorders such as borderline personality disorder (BPD)

Impulsivity

Impulsivity symptoms continue to influence ADHD behavior in women. Impulsivity is associated with:

- gender-typical behaviors, including behaviors perceived as controlling, demanding, irritable, etc.
- risky behaviors such as speeding and extreme sports
- addictive behaviors, including substance abuse and gambling
- a significantly increased likelihood of reacting to negative emotions, including self-harm (skin picking, cutting, etc.)

How To Recognize ADHD In Women

Gender-specific words are used in this section to refer to people who identify as female and who have the typical reproductive organs of a cisgender woman. We recognize that some people who identify as female may not have the anatomy described in this here.

Attention Deficit Hyperactivity Disorder (ADHD) is a neurodevelopmental disorder characterized by symptoms of inattention, hyperactivity, and impulsivity. Studies show that ADHD is more common in men than women, but new research suggests that ADHD is underdiagnosed in women and women tend to be diagnosed later than men. The prevalence of ADHD may be more equal between men and women than previously thought.

Greater awareness of how ADHD behaves differently in girls and women than in boys and men leads to more ADHD diagnoses in girls, although differences still exist.

How ADHD Differs Between Women and Men

Girls and women show more inattention than hyperactivity/impulsivity. They also show more symptoms of internalizing than externalizing. Because these symptoms are less bothersome and don't fit the ADHD stereotype, ADHD in girls is often overlooked.

Girls can often develop coping strategies that mask their ADHD symptoms, especially when they are younger. When they have noticeable symptoms, other conditions, such as anxiety or depression (both are common conditions in girls and women with ADHD), rather than being accurately diagnosed with ADHD.

Studies have shown that teachers are less likely to refer girls for ADHD assessment, which can delay diagnosis and treatment.

When assessed, girls and women tend to meet fewer of the diagnostic criteria described in the Diagnostic and Statistical Manual of Mental Disorders (DSM-5) for ADHD, as these criteria were developed from predominantly male samples. These delays in diagnosis and treatment often hinder the basic skills learned in primary school and can lead to a decline in the academic and psychosocial performance of girls and women.

Symptoms Of ADHD In Girls And Women Are Usually:

- Belongs to the inattentive category (although girls and women can also have hyperactive/impulsive symptoms)
- Appears weaker than in boys and men
- Being penetrating and obstructive rather than transient or vacillating
- Appears later, often during a social or school transition
- Adult women find they need assessment and treatment (rather than referral)

Hormonal changes such as puberty, menstruation, pregnancy, and menopause reinforce.

Diagnostic Considerations and Challenges

Doctors use DSM-5 guidelines to diagnose ADHD, along with rating scales, interviews, and other methods. Research shows that, compared to boys and men, girls and women are consistently diagnosed and underdiagnosed with ADHD based on this diagnostic criteria. The reasons for this difference are as follows.

1. Attentional presentation of symptoms

- The ADHD experiences of many women and girls, which do not seem to bother others, are characterized by a subtle presentation of symptoms, with a greater likelihood of being overlooked. However, many physicians are more familiar with the overactive and disruptive manifestations of ADHD, which are more common in men and boys. Research shows that hyperactivity and impulsivity and other outward symptoms (such as conduct problems) are strong predictors of diagnosis compared to other ADHD presentations.

- Camouflaging symptoms: Studies show that women are highly motivated to hide and compensate for their ADHD symptoms. The symptoms seen are often related to anxiety or mood, which can lead to misdiagnosis.

2. Gender Bias

- Although it is seldom deliberate, gender prejudice is sneaky and persistent. It impacts the way physicians categorize and see women.
- Referrals: Insignificant, unobtrusive symptoms are rarely a cause for concern, so few girls and adolescents with such symptoms are referred for diagnosis or counseling.

ADHD rating scales are always biased towards male behavioral symptoms. Internal symptoms and limitations are often overlooked and many tools are not standardized to women's values.

3. Hormonal influence

Ovarian hormones interact with nearly every system in the body and are important components of the physical, social, and emotional health of all women. The brain is a target organ for estrogen because it protects the brain by increasing neurotransmitter activity, which in turn affects executive function, attention, motivation, verbal memory, sleep, and concentration.

Estrogen levels, which vary both month-to-month and across the lifespan, influence the severity of ADHD symptoms in women. ADHD is generally thought of as a disease with stable symptoms over time, but women and their bodies are not. The truth is:

- ADHD symptoms vary with hormonal fluctuations. ADHD symptoms increase when estrogen decreases. Estrogen levels drop after ovulation, in the middle of the cycle, and even more at the start of menstruation. This combination of low estrogen and high progesterone makes symptoms much worse. It also means that symptoms can vary from day to day. Some women may even be more sensitive to these micro-vibrations.

- Estrogen begins during puberty when ADHD symptoms become more pronounced in girls. These hormonal changes often manifest as anxiety and emotional volatility, but they can also increase during this time, leading to misdiagnosis of an anxiety or mood disorder and incorrect or inadequate treatment.

Treatment Considerations

ADHD can be managed with therapy, medication, lifestyle changes, and housing. Women with ADHD should consider the following treatment options:

- A doctor and/or therapist with experience with ADHD in women and girls. Finding that professional is perhaps the most important and difficult of all. Be sure to ask about their experiences with treating ADHD in women.
- Family psychoeducation: It is important that your support network also includes ADHD.
- Reframing: Therapists can help you validate your experiences, question the impact of societal expectations on your outlook, and learn how to stand up for yourself.

- Medications: It is important to find a doctor who understands the effects of hormones on ADHD and how they interact with medications. For example, stimulants may be less effective in the second half of the menstrual cycle. Hormone replacement therapy significantly improves ADHD symptoms in postmenopausal women because it increases available estrogen and progesterone. SSRIs are commonly prescribed for anxiety and mood disorders, so doctors need to understand how stimulants interact with SSRIs and affect overall symptoms.

- Environment Restructuring: Therapists and other professionals can help you rearrange your environment to better suit your needs, thoughts, and life.

Chapter 4.

ADHD, Women, And The Risk Of Emotional Withdrawal

Attention deficit hyperactivity disorder and emotional withdrawal; pulling away from friends, strangers, and loved ones often go hand in hand. Many women with ADHD adopt withdrawal as a coping mechanism after experiencing rejection, disappointment, and bullying their entire lives. It's difficult to break this bad behavior, yet your relationships may depend on it.

My husband keeps talking but I don't listen. I turn away from him. He, in turn, said or did something completely innocent on his end

- commented on the need to do laundry, said he was too tired for sex, gently teased me that I was in love with a movie star and I am finished. You see, my ADHD and emotional withdrawal are caused by my rejection sensitivity or my rejection sensitivity dysphoria (RSD), which can cause me to misinterpret things as a referendum on my (now perceived) general abhorrence. as a person. The cauldron of guilt and anger, shame and misery can be overwhelming. So, I turn around. I return to myself, I shut myself down emotionally.

Emotional withdrawal is a learned behavior

Girls with ADHD often learn emotional withdrawal at an early age: in women, ADHD and emotional withdrawal often go hand in hand.

We can slowly pick up on the social cues that other girls pick up easily. We're dreamy and expansive, rarely grounded in the here and now (probably because the here and now means forgotten papers, missed deadlines, and people asking why we're not doing better). Our organization itself can make us a social pariah as other students try to distance themselves from the "bad" child. We often argue impulsively at inappropriate times, which others have noticed may attract the attention of the bully.

As if the social ostracism of "average girls" wasn't enough, girls with ADHD are often actively bullied and in the 1980s and 1990s, nobody did much but tell us that it was so serious. If the boy had been bullied, the authority figure would have said, "Oh, he only does it because he loves you." (Create the conditions so that we can later confuse abuse with healthy relationships).

We were often our only allies. Our teachers and parents may have dismissed our complaints as nagging or, like mine, dismissed them with something like, "If you had learned to behave like everyone else, this wouldn't happen to you." We have learned to blame ourselves for our own exclusion; we were not worthy of belonging to social groups or for the popularity of other students.

So, we interrupted. We learned that we don't care because it hurts too much to care. When the teasing started, when the bullying started (again), and when the spitballs started flying, we moved in. It was the only coping mechanism we had.

We Carry The Emotional Baggage Of ADHD Into Adulthood

Emotional withdrawal means you suppress your emotions. It's about cutting off people who can help us because we're so used to rejection that we've learned to anticipate it. Because we have learned to separate ourselves from others, we develop other unhealthy coping mechanisms.

Studies also show what we encounter. Teenage girls with ADHD are more likely to have social, attention, and organizational problems; have a poorer self-image; experience more mental stress and disabilities; and have less control over their lives. Women with ADHD are also 2.5 times more likely to experience extreme grief than women without ADHD.

These are pretty grim circumstances. And a lot of that stems from our need to "shut down" our emotions or shut down how we feel when interacting with the world around us. We have learned to anticipate constant crises, so we have developed unhealthy coping mechanisms – some of which evolve into full-fledged psychiatric disorders to function in a neurotypical world. We are always afraid of making a mistake, missing a social signal, or missing an important deadline. And not all the planners in this world can help us.

This is why women with ADHD withdraw

We leave. Above all, the most dangerously, we distance ourselves from those we love because they probably hurt us the most. Some research has suggested that the divorce rate for couples with one or more partners with ADHD is twice that of the general population. This may be due in part to ADHD and sex-related complications, inattentiveness, "busy wars" and time management errors. But as one woman put it, "I have often thought about pulling away because I can't stand criticism. She thinks she's helping me to be a better person" when she finds that her flaws related to ADD are "unloved".

How Can We Respond Positively To Emotional Withdrawal?

First, admit that you withdraw from people and situations as a coping mechanism. It can be hard to admit because it's been the only way to deal with it for so long. But recognition is the first step. Learn to say when you turn away from your partner or friends, "I turn away and I'm shaking in this situation. I'm losing strength." It requires extensive, hard labor. In other words, you must first grasp what is occurring and go over your emotional responses. An excellent first step in the correct path is to be able to say to yourself, "I'm emotionally withdrawing now."

Declare what's happening, even if it might be frightening. Recalling the related script is beneficial. It may be a straightforward matter: "I've got ADHD. As a coping technique, I mastered withdrawal. When you did x, I felt like I had to withdraw to protect myself. " That doesn't mean you should or shouldn't opt out. This means that your partner (probably your spouse) needs to know what's going on. He won't feel like he's to blame because you based him on your own learned behavior and hopefully you can work together to calm yourself down and help him.

Then sit down and make a list. What could have happened instead of withdrawing? You may want to be reassured that your feelings matter. You may prefer to give verbal assurances that you are loved just the way you are. Maybe you want a hug. If you're shy about it or don't feel like it, you might want your hand. Brainstorm a list of your partner's behaviors that can make you feel safer, then share it with them. Don't blame; instead, give constructive advice on how to help yourself with emotional dissociation.

Get Professional Help

Are you currently in therapy? You should be. We have seen that women who "shut down" their emotions by experiencing painfully inappropriate emotional responses can lead to a host of negative outcomes.

A good cognitive behavioral therapist can help you develop more coping mechanisms to help you deal with your emotions. You learn how to change your irrational thought patterns - in this case, the idea that direct feedback or input from other people destroys your self-esteem - into more positive ones, and how to deal with negative thoughts when they arise: do not stand on them, standstill, or stop them.

There are several ways to find a good therapist. Someone who offers CBT (cognitive-behavioral therapy) or DBT (dialectical behavior therapy, a form of CBT) with an ADHD specialty is preferred. These professionals can help you stop your emotional withdrawal and learn healthier, less dangerous coping mechanisms that can improve your relationships instead of sabotaging them.

Emotional withdrawal can damage your relationships, disrupt your marriage, and sabotage your life through unhealthy coping mechanisms. But you can free yourself from its grip. Emotional withdrawal is a behavior that many women with ADHD have learned through rejection, fear, and intimidation. it may take time, therapy, and help to overcome it. It is important to have a strong support network (including, if possible, an understanding partner) and a good therapist.

But above all, you need a strong commitment to change. Without it, you'll get stuck in the old withdrawal rut: and it won't help anyone, let alone yourself.

Chapter 5.

ADHD In Older Women

For women who have ignored ADHD since childhood, symptoms of inattention may be more noticeable in structured educational settings such as high school, college, or university. Coping strategies used to compensate for symptoms in younger grades may be more difficult to maintain in these situations.

As with girls with ADHD, older women with ADHD tend to have more inattentive and internalized symptoms. Among them:

- Difficulty paying attention to details / making "wrong mistakes".
- Difficulty concentrating on long tasks or engaging in activities that require sustained mental effort (writing reports, filling out forms, looking at long papers, etc.)
- It's hard to listen well when someone is talking
- Difficulty following instructions or completing tasks
- Organizational issues such as time management, workplace/home cleanliness, or organizing tasks and activities
- Commonly misplaced everyday items such as keys, wallets, phones, etc.
- Easily distracted by incoherent thoughts or stimuli
- Forgetfulness in daily activities such as paying bills, meeting deadlines, going to scheduled meetings, or calling back
- Difficulty making realistic and manageable plans
- Difficulty making decisions
- Postponing/doing things at the last minute
- Difficulty regulating emotions, especially under stress

Hyperactive/impulsive symptoms are less common than inattention, both in women and in adults in general. These symptoms often become more "internal" if they persist. Hyperactive/impulsive symptoms that adult women may experience include:

- Restlessness/difficulty sitting still for long periods (unsteadiness, tapping hands or feet, rolling over in a chair, getting up, etc.)
- Talks excessively or has difficulty staying calm during recreational activities
- Answer questions before they are asked, interrupt or disturb others
- Issues with waiting for a turn, queuing, etc.

Women With ADHD Are More Likely Than Women Without ADHD To Have:

- poor self-image
- They have co-occurring illnesses such as anxiety and depression
- The feelings of lack of control over situations

- Difficulties with personal/professional life
- Physical symptoms such as headaches, stomach aches, and/or trouble sleeping
- Have communication and relationship problems

How ADHD Affects Motherhood

Some women with ADHD note that symptoms such as lightheadedness and difficulty resuming a task after a break became more pronounced when they became mothers. For many, having children brings additional challenges and concerns that ADHD can affect their children.

Treatment For ADHD Symptoms In Women

Medications are usually the first line of treatment for ADHD. There are two classes of drugs used to treat ADHD: *stimulants and non-stimulants.*

Stimulants are more common and generally considered more effective. They include:

64

Non-amphetamines: methylphenidate (MPH), dexmethylphenidate (dexMPH)

Amphetamine: Dextroamphetamine (dexAMP)

Mixed Amphetamine Salts (MAS-XR)

Non-stimulants are used when stimulants do not adequately control symptoms or when stimulants are not tolerated or are contraindicated. Among them:

- Atomoxetine (ATX)
- Guanfacine extended-release
- Clonidine HCL extended release

Despite its effectiveness, research suggests that girls and women with ADHD are less likely to be prescribed ADHD medications than boys and men, although ADHD medication use appears to be increasing among women.

Some research suggests that girls and women may react differently to ADHD medications than boys and men. Further research may provide suggestions for personalized treatment.

There is no evidence that women should receive different drug treatments for ADHD, but doctors should consider comorbidities and potential drug interactions.

Therapy for ADHD

In addition to medication, it can be helpful to participate in ADHD-focused treatments that address a variety of issues such as self-esteem, interpersonal and family relationships, health habits, stress levels, and skills. of life. Although it can be difficult, it is important to find a therapist who has knowledge and experience in treating girls and women with ADHD.

Some Treatments That May Be Helpful Include:

Cognitive Behavioral Therapy: The goal of cognitive behavioral therapy (CBT) is to recognize and alter unhelpful or unhelpful (negative) thoughts and actions. Can handle emotional self-regulation, impulse control, and stress management. Can often be modified to address existing conditions alongside ADHD. CBT programs designed specifically for adults with ADHD are available.

Neurocognitive psychotherapy: combines aspects of CBT and cognitive rehabilitation to support the development of life skills to improve cognitive function, learn compensatory strategies, and reorganize the environment.

Dialectical Behavior Therapy (DBT): Uses strategies such as radical acceptance, mindfulness, and emotion regulation to help people learn and break free from ADHD thought and response patterns.

ADHD treatment should be started as soon as ADHD is diagnosed, even in young children.

Chapter 6

The Transformative Power Of An ADHD Diagnosis For Older Women

G etting an ADHD diagnosis (let alone treatment) is extremely healing and life-changing. This is the damning message I heard from the dozens of women I interviewed, all over the age of 60, who were diagnosed with ADHD later in life. Here are solutions to the top five challenges women with ADHD face.

Regret is a common (and understandable) response to a diagnosis of Attention Deficit Hyperactivity Disorder (ADHD) later in life. Some newly diagnosed people lament how undiagnosed ADHD has disrupted their lives and derailed them. They are angry, bitter, and saddened by the blame and shame of recent years.

But many, many more feel relief as the main response to an ADHD diagnosis — and the answers it brings. For them, a late diagnosis strengthens their resolve and fundamentally changes their path and outlook for the better.

These are the experiences of approximately 75 women I interviewed*, all aged 60 and over, who were diagnosed with ADHD at a later age. They describe what led up to their diagnosis and how learning about ADHD helps them deal with the challenges associated with it that still haunt them today.

The ADHD Turning Point

What drives women to be diagnosed with ADHD later in life? Increased awareness of the disease, especially among women, is a common trigger. Many women also seek help when daily demands at some point become too much for them or when the hormonal changes of menopause exacerbate symptoms.

Here is what the women told me:

- "I excelled throughout my time as an ER nurse. After that, I was given a desk job, which was awful. I lost my job because I was unable to keep up. My boss described me as forgetful and unorganized. I then sought treatment for ADHD. Since I've worked as a therapist, I believe I've had ADHD for around 20 years. At the age of 60, I tried to start my own practice but had great difficulty due to the lack of structure. I then decided it was time to get a formal diagnosis.
- "I had a lot of clutter issues. I was in a cleaning class and the trainer mentioned ADHD."
- "I attended counseling. I was given a book on ADHD by my sister, and I was able to identify many of the symptoms in myself."

While the challenges of undiagnosed ADHD are enormous, it sometimes takes decades to diagnose, in part because women feel pressured to conform to societal norms – from primary breadwinner to detail-oriented friend who does everything. Keep this in mind - which is often at odds with the nature of ADHD.

In psychology, we say ADHD is ego-dystonic for women because it contradicts our personal ideals and expectations. (I'm also a woman with ADHD.) In other words, ADHD makes us feel bad as women. This could explain why women with ADHD experience anxiety more often than their male counterparts.

Post-Diagnosis: Clarity, Acceptance, and Hope

Indeed, some women have tearfully expressed regret over their ADHD diagnosis, associating the once undiagnosed condition with failed marriages, friendships, and careers, as well as difficulty raising a child (often alone) and other painful experiences.

But most of the women I interviewed acknowledged that their diagnosis was transformative, exciting, and insightful. This motivated them to discover original coping mechanisms and study more about ADHD. More significantly, their new understanding prompted self-acceptance:

- "I have experienced a very pleasant sense of re-energization. I can control my thoughts enough to not dwell too much on my childhood struggles, and I am still grateful to be alive and learning right now.

- "I now understand that my problems with planning, time management, procrastination, and motivation are not signs of character flaws. I have far less negative self-talk.

- I'm much more confident in myself. I feel like I'm changing. I accept and embrace my ADHD now that I am aware of it. Others may object to it, but that is their issue. I now embrace who I am.

Top Difficulties Cited By Older Women With ADHD

Even after a diagnosis, ADHD is not without ongoing challenges. Some women have noticed that they put all their energy into their careers and "mask" ADHD at work, to the detriment of family and other aspects of life. Others reported financial difficulties and admitted they would be a mess if their husbands weren't there.

No matter the challenge, I always recommend the following:

- Find or create an environment that is much more supportive of what you need.
- Ask yourself: "How can I improve the quality, enjoyment, and fulfillment of my life?"

Below are the most common problems associated with ADHD later in life, according to the women I interviewed, followed by suggested solutions.

ADHD Challenge #1: Getting Things Done

Procrastination, low motivation, lack of focus, and lack of self-discipline plague older women, especially in retirement.

Solutions

- **Reevaluate your motivation.** Are your tasks on the to-do list driven by must-haves? Does your list match what you really want to do? Your list and stress level can only change based on your answers. Never be hesitant to pursue your own goals. You have the right to deviate from the standards set generations ago.

- **Look out for simplicity.** Those of us with ADHD often create far too much complexity in our lives. (Part of this has to do with impulsivity.) Order quiets the brain. Think about the activities, objects, and other parts of your day that you enjoy and those that disappoint you. I tried not to have too many plans for a day, as one interviewee said. I used to write lists, and when nothing happened, I became frantic. Now I tell myself, "I'll do my best."
- Realize that it always takes conscious effort to get things done, but it pays to lead an orderly life.

ADHD Challenge #2: Social Issues

"People" — whether they're saying the wrong thing and talking too much or missing social cues — are especially annoying to women, who are hardwired for social relationships. The resulting pain of feeling misunderstood weighs heavily on this group.

Solutions

- Join a support group. Social connection is one of the most healing experiences we can have as women with ADHD. I have seen older women in the support groups I have led over the years (both online and in person) find acceptance, safety, companionship, and validation in a way that they had never known before.

ADHD Challenge #3: Emotional Disorder

From irritability and anxiety to breakdowns and rejection sensitivity, the women I spoke to the reported emotional turmoil that disrupts relationships and daily life.

Solutions

- Emotional dysregulation is a natural and important part of ADHD. Few people know that ADHD also affects emotions. In my opinion, it is necessary to see ADHD as a self-regulation disorder before starting to develop emotional regulation skills.
- Assess your triggers. What stresses you out? What tensions do you experience that discourage you? Even identifying a few pain points can make a difference.

ADHD Challenge #4: Time Management

Older people experience the following problems with this classic ADHD pain point:

- Time blindness
- Inflexibility
- Failing to establish and maintain a daily routine

Solutions

- find the structure. Its absence is almost always the cause of time management problems. Start small with a few anchors - bedtime, mealtime, etc. Some seniors may benefit from living in a seniors' community where structures are created for them. (I consider it an adult summer camp.)

ADHD Challenge #5: Restlessness

Physical hyperactivity decreases with age, but inner restlessness remains. Women told me they had to do one thing (or things) all the time and couldn't sit still or relax. As a result, they often took on too much and left projects unfinished. Hyperactivity also manifests as rapid thinking - a major cause of sleep problems.

Solutions

- Practice moderation. You have more time for your hobbies and interests than you think. Channel your ambition and anxiety in a few small steps at a time. Instead of buying 200 flower bulbs to plant in your garden, start with a small flower bed. If you would want more, you can always get it.
- Focus on one thing to calm racing thoughts before bed. For example, listen to a podcast when you're comfortable in bed with the lights off.
- Remember that no matter how old we are, we are always incomplete. In our latter years, there are many things we may learn to adjust to improve the quality and satisfaction of our lives.

Chapter 7.

Why A Basic Assessment Is Critical And Comprehensive Lifestyle Changes Can Most Help With ADHD Treatment.

Questions And Answers

Older people suffer unnecessarily from undiagnosed ADHD. This is unfortunate – and sadly common, as many medical professionals are not trained to recognize ADHD in patients over 50, even if they show a clear pattern of behavior and symptoms.

This lack of awareness and education goes beyond the diagnosis and effective treatment of this demographic. Learn about the importance of screening for Attention Deficit Hyperactivity Disorder (ADHD or ADD) in older adults, as well as evidence-based treatments and lifestyle interventions in this Q&A session with Kathleen Nadeau, Ph.D., director of the Chesapeake ADHD Center at Bethesda. Maryland.

Q: What Is The Best Way To Find A Doctor Who Specializes In ADHD In The Elderly?

It is not easy. Larger urban areas tend to have strong ADHD clinics. If you are out of town, it is a good idea to get a formal assessment in such a place and return it to your GP for further treatment, especially if he or she does not feel qualified to assess you or if he is reluctant to do so. These forms outline the diagnostic procedure and recommended treatment for the individual.

It is also important to note that no one truly expert in diagnosing ADHD in older adults will limit the diagnosis to DSM-V alone, as the ADHD symptoms that exist are primarily for children and do not reflect the attentional experience of adults. a deficiency for the most part.

As a patient, I would question doctors who rely too much on understanding the symptoms of ADHD in children. If other people like relatives can talk about it, it is useful information. But most of the time, interviews from the distant past probably give the wrong answers. Which memory is right 60 years later? Additionally, the onset of symptoms can vary over the years, and lifestyle factors can do a lot to "mask" ADHD symptoms.

Q: Speaking Of Symptoms, Can Menopause Complicate Diagnosis Later In Life?

We know that the brain is a target organ for estrogen. This means that when estrogen levels fluctuate, our dopamine and serotonin receptors – which are involved in attention, self-control, anxiety, and mood disorders – are less sensitive. We also know that, on average, estrogen levels begin to decline around age 40, and this decline over several years can significantly worsen ADHD symptoms. Overall, there is enough evidence to suggest a link between estrogen and ADHD symptoms, and we need more research on this link.

Q: What Treatments And Interventions Are Best For Seniors With ADHD?

One of the first things I talk to elderly patients about after a diagnosis is learning daily brain-friendly habits that improve health and cognition. This includes:

- **Sleep:** Recent studies show that at certain stages of deep sleep, our brain is cleansed of toxins that can cause, for example, Alzheimer's disease. Adequate sleep is essential for overall health and functioning.
- **Nutrition:** I always advise patients to eat low glycemic foods, limit starches and sugars, and eat protein at every meal. This combination ensures a steady supply of glucose that our brain uses.
- **Stress management**
- **Education**

Structure and social interaction are also important for older people with ADHD. It's important to stay connected to others because healthy relationships improve our mood and ability to focus. I advise my patients to actively pursue social engagement via hobbies and networking. One way to achieve this is through nursing homes, where social life and activities are integrated. Some seniors may also benefit from retirement.

Professional executive coaching is also a great way to encourage structure by working on day-to-day issues such as problem-solving, habit-building, time management, organization, money management, etc.

Q: What about stimulants? Can they be safely prescribed to older people to treat ADHD?

In my experience, many adults can tolerate and benefit from stimulants. For people with cardiovascular problems, approval from a family doctor or cardiologist is required before prescribing stimulants (this applies to ADHD patients of all ages). We are also starting to print at a very low dose.

In general, many psychiatrists and general practitioners are reluctant to prescribe stimulants, and often for no good reason. They are usually concerned about the interaction between stimulants and other medications, as older people are more likely to take multiple medications, or about the effects of stimulants on the heart. I find this ironic because it is not uncommon in geriatric medicine to prescribe stimulants to wake up and energize the brain.

Often advice and documentation from an outside ADHD clinic (as noted above) are enough to persuade the GP to prescribe stimulants. When stimulants don't work, older people can also benefit from non-stimulants.

Q: Is there a significant benefit to being diagnosed with ADHD later in life?

There are huge benefits to being diagnosed at any point in life, but this is especially true later on. I sometimes hear people make archaic statements like, "Why does it matter if you have ADHD?" You are 72 years old. But it is important; Proper diagnosis and treatment have a major impact on quality of life.

Living with undiagnosed ADHD makes life more stressful and makes people feel uncomfortable. Diagnosis alone is therapeutic and allows us to help older people restructure their lives. My advice to older people who think they have ADHD is to stop rejecting themselves.

Chapter 8.

Why ADHD Treatment Gets Tougher With Age

A woman living in the rural south heard about my research on the elderly and ADHD (ADHD or ADD) and contacted me with a sincere request for help. Marjorie had read about ADHD in adults in her 50s and quickly realized that many patterns of ADHD matched her own life experience.

Like many adults with ADHD, Marjorie has lived a long and eventful life with many jobs, including that of a part-time college professor. She and her husband lived and tended the family farm.

The downside is that you don't have access to ADHD medication.

He was a very resourceful person and would do anything to get a formal diagnosis from a clinical psychologist two hours away from the farm. Then, through his network of friends and acquaintances, he found a doctor in a remote area who prescribed him stimulants at the age of 50. As he described it, "a light turned on" when he started using stimulants. Suddenly he saw the tasks in front of him, prioritized them, and started completing each task. His story has been an ADHD success story.

Still, he found a psychologist, got an accurate diagnosis, and found a local doctor willing to prescribe stimulants. Thus begins a fruitful collaboration between Marjorie and her doctor which will last several years.

Seventeen years later, however, their success story has crumbled. The doctor who had been his doctor announced his resignation. Now in her late 60s, Marjorie was looking for a new doctor, but couldn't find anyone who would consider treating a woman her own age. Some did not believe that ADHD existed in older people. Some didn't think he could have ADHD because he had a graduate degree. Others wouldn't take the "risk" they saw in prescribing stimulants to an elderly person at risk of developing heart or other complications.

Older people are losing their ADHD treatment options

All this led him to approach me. "What should I do?" He asked. - Managing a farm with my husband is not an easy task. There are things I have to worry about from morning till night and I quickly fall back into the confusing place where I lived for so long before I started using stimulants. Also, my mother was 95 years old. I couldn't imagine functioning for another 25 years without the aid of stimulants."

Although Marjorie's challenge of accessing care was complicated by living in a rural area, seniors across the country face this challenge every day. As a result, we have a large and growing group of adults over the age of 60 who were diagnosed with ADHD in their 40s who have benefited from stimulants and found that treatment options close with age.

Also, adults who are diagnosed later in life may face a bigger problem. Some doctors are willing to prescribe stimulants to people who have had prescriptions before, but newly diagnosed seniors are skeptical. "Why do you even worry about ADHD at your age?" a lot of questions.

- Find a doctor who knows about ADHD
- If younger members of your family (children or grandchildren) are being treated for ADHD, contact your doctor and make an appointment. This medical professional is certainly aware of the high genetic nature of ADHD and the likelihood that medications can benefit you and your offspring.
- Be active in your local CHADD group and help start a local support group for seniors. There is the power of numbers. The more providers you research, the better your chances of finding one.
- Consider going to a major metropolitan area where it may be easier to find a supplier. Begin treatment with this provider with a plan to seek treatment locally once the diagnosis and positive response to medications are confirmed.

Chapter 9.

How To Retire With ADHD: Structure, Stimulation, Goals

After retirement, many people with ADHD spend their time in the wrong places: online shopping, daytime TV, and restaurants. Use these strategies to create a more fulfilling life after leaving full-time work.

Retirement is surprisingly difficult. Our working years give us daily structure, an integrated social life, and purpose. Once these have disappeared, retirement leaves a void that is difficult to fill.

If you retire with ADHD (ADHD or ADD), the challenge is even greater. We love structure and stimulation, but struggle to create it ourselves. Many of us resort to the "standard" stimulation: overeating, drinking too much alcohol, shopping online, overusing social media and watching too much TV.

How do you create structure, find healthy sources of inspiration, and maintain meaning in retirement? I've spoken to many retirees with ADHD and here are their strategies:

1. Work Part-Time.

Sally worked as a high school art teacher for many years while raising two daughters as a single mother. Her house might not have been the prettiest and her weeknight dinners were a little hit or miss, but caring for her daughters and going to work during the week gave her the structure she needed to counteract her ADHD.

When she retired, she moved to a community near her eldest daughter. But instead of feeling happy, she felt lost. Her daughter suggested she take art classes at a local community center. One thing leads to another. When the staff at the community center learned that Sally was a retired art teacher, they invited her to teach classes.

The community center became her home for social activities and part-time work, giving her recognition, a valued role, and a dedication to an activity she had always loved.

2. Be Active In A Church Community.

Many seniors I speak to say that their church community has become the center of their social life. For some, that means weekly church attendance and maybe some sort of midweek group. Those with higher energy levels and a greater need for stimulation are involved in church activities.

The key is to consider ADHD when deciding what to volunteer for. Roles that require planning and organizational skills may not be suitable. Those who need to dive in and help with an already established activity generally perform better. Mary loves to garden and has volunteered to maintain the landscape around her church. She pulls weeds, mows, and plants flowers, but is not involved in setting up the management of Church property.

3. Voluntary.

Finding meaningful volunteer activities can be difficult, especially for those who are in a career and are looking for responsibility and stimulation. One approach is to identify an organization whose mission you support and contact them to see if you can add value to their organization. A woman I know, a retired English teacher, volunteers at the local juvenile detention center, where she started a popular reading group. She reports that the young inmates are some of the most enthusiastic and dedicated students she has ever had.

4. Take Courses Designed For Seniors.

When you have ADHD, good intentions disappear when there is no structure to help you get started and move on. You may dream of learning Italian or writing a dissertation, but the key to such projects is structure. Many communities have classes specifically for seniors. You may want to develop stronger computer skills. The structure required to keep a senior with ADHD on track may be found in organized courses.

5. Be A Part Of A Group For Active Adults.

Seniors with ADHD often thrive in communities with energetic adults. These often provide a variety of events, clubs, and activities. You just need to show up; there is nothing to arrange or prepare. It's ideal for seniors who are interested in a variety of things but find it difficult to plan events or connect with others who share their interests. It resembles a senior summer camp.

6. Phased Retirement.

Some of us have the option of gradually reducing our working hours or changing the way we work in retirement. Self-employed people have more control over the phased retirement process.

Hank had worked in the family business for almost 30 years. The business was sold on the understanding that Hank would stay on if needed to mentor and train the new owners and introduce them to the business' regular customers. At first, Hank was frustrated with this turn of events, but after a few months, he realized it was a win-win deal. He had time to plan exciting trips, including a long bike ride he had always dreamed of and was comfortable in his new role with the old company. He maintained his expert identity while dipping his toe into the retreat.

Resources: Tips And Tools For Treating ADHD

- Accept your ADHD
- Take your time to make decisions
- Know your limits and practice them
- Develop strong self-care habits
- Use of coping tools (Like an ADHD planner) and strategies to cope with everyday life
- Find a community or support group
- Prioritize the things you really love
- Seek professional help (multimodal treatment: medication to treat symptoms and behavioral therapy to develop skills and strategies needed to minimize disability)

Printed in Great Britain
by Amazon

35993373R00056